# CONTEN

# The
# Practice
## *of*
# Enchantment

*The*

# Practice

*of*

# Enchantment

MYTHBLAST ESSAYS, 2020-2024

JOANNA GARDNER

JOSEPH CAMPBELL
FOUNDATION

Paperback ISBN: 978-1-61178-043-7

Ebook ISBN: 978-1-61178-044-4

Front cover image detail from "Starry Night Over the Rhone" by Vincent van Gogh

Book design by *the*BookDesigners

First printing edition 2024

www.jcf.org

*For my mother,*
*who first enchanted everything,*
*and for all the grandmothers*

# *In* SEARCH *of* ENCHANTMENT

In a world of jobs and drudgery, it can be all too easy to lose touch with enchantment.

Hold on—enchantment? Isn't that for story books and silly kids? The more you grow up, the more enchantment fades from your world. Right?

Maybe. But maybe not. Especially when you manage to see your own personal journey through a filter of mythic metaphor, as through myth-vision goggles.

## MAX WEBER AND THE ABSENCE OF ENCHANTMENT

The "disenchantment of the world" is one of the most enduring phrases in the writings of the German scholar Max Weber (1864-1920), one of the founding voices in the field of sociology and in the wider project of critical theory.[1] Weber's work has been enormously influential in academia, and he mused upon the idea of disenchantment often throughout his career,[2] including in a talk he gave to a group of students.

It was November of 1917. Autumn was giving way to winter. A previously inconceivable world war was staggering to its inglorious end, and Germany was about to lose. Weber himself, fifty-three years old at the time, had spent almost twenty years swinging between, on one hand, extreme depression and anxiety and on the other, "manic spurts of extraordinarily intense intellectual work."[3] Add it all up, and he had well-founded reasons to feel glum.

Here's what Weber told those students at that moment in history:

> The fate of our times is characterized by rationalization and intellectualization and, above all, by the 'disenchantment of the world.' Precisely the ultimate and most sublime values have retreated from public life either into the transcendental realm of mystic life or into the brotherliness of direct and personal human relations.[4]

Disenchantment *above all*? Weber is not mincing words here. Perhaps that explains, in part, why his observation struck such a chord. Legions of commenters since then, including yours truly, have weighed in on the idea, teasing apart enchantment, disenchantment, and re-enchantment from many different perspectives.[5]

It seems, however, impossible to ignore that grand, sweeping phrase, "disenchantment of the world." It lands with the persuasive weight of gravity. I can feel my shoulders slump in its force field, and I feel a temptation to respond with defeated resignation: *Oh, right. Of course the world is disenchanted. Anything else would be folly.*

But I don't think Weber was saying the whole world is disenchanted. For one thing, he clearly uses the word "world" figuratively and not literally here, because as the passage goes on to say, the world does in fact contain enchantment. Enchantment, he suggests, or the "ultimate and most sublime values" haven't left the world completely but have left the public sphere, and can now be found in two less-public spheres: mysticism and relationships, or in other words, spirituality and love.

And maybe, whether he realized it or not, Weber was also saying that *his* world was disenchanted. Beginning in his teens, Weber flung himself into scholarly work—intellectualization, as he calls it—with a fever-pitch zeal, structuring his professional life around thinking and theorizing.[6] He even equated his value as a person with his work: "He felt that only a man at his work is a full man."[7] Once, soon after he began his first teaching post, his wife Marianne mentioned that maybe sleeping might be an idea to consider once in a while, and he replied, "If I don't work until one o'clock I can't be a professor."[8] Work, work, work, and then work some more. How could this driven, lopsided focus on intellect and rationality *not* lead to disenchantment?

Sure enough, four years later, at the young age of thirty-four, in the wake of overwork and overthinking, Weber experienced an acute nervous breakdown from which he never fully recovered. That was when his struggles with depression and anxiety began. He died at fifty-six, two and a half years after delivering the talk I quoted from above. In that passage, I can't help but hear a self-diagnosis as much as a sociological one. Marked by what we might today call workaholism and burnout, Weber's world was more cursed than enchanted. Which brings us to myth and Joseph Campbell.

## THE MAVERICK ENCHANTMENT
## OF JOSEPH CAMPBELL

If Max Weber suffered in the absence of enchantment, Joseph Campbell (1904-1987) seems to have flourished in its embrace. Where Weber's personal motto might have been "Get to work!", Campbell's was "Follow your bliss." At least that seems to have been how he lived his life. Those three words, *follow your bliss*, can, I think, function as a north star that leads on to enchantment.

Campbell's instinct for bliss and therefore enchantment began early in his life. When graduate studies failed to help him find his "center,"[9] as he called it, Campbell chose not to complete a PhD. Instead, he heeded his intuition and embarked upon his own reading program, following bliss straight into the enchanted heart of myth and its many metaphors. After a few years of this, at the age of thirty, coincidentally the same age as which Max Weber became a professor, Campbell began teaching myth at Sarah Lawrence College.

Unlike Weber, however, Joseph Campbell read, wrote, taught, and lectured zestfully, energetically, and steadily for another fifty-three years, and his ideas still resonate today, inspiring students and creative people from all walks of life. He created a career as a mythologist, unreservedly devoting himself to his heart's passion. He was lucky, certainly, but somehow his work was also sustainable and perhaps even sustaining, where Weber's seems to have been more devouring. I suspect this has to do with the centered nature of the ideas that Campbell lived and shared with his students.

One of Campbell's most centered concepts, I think, is his four functions of myth. Instead of reading myth literally, he championed metaphorical interpretations of these sacred stories, and his four functions describe four important metaphors he found in mythic images. Although ostensibly applying to the macrocosm of mythology, Campbell's four functions can also reflect and reinforce a personal sense of balance and wholeness.

He describes the four functions many times, but a representative example is in Chapter Five of his book, *Pathways to Bliss: Mythology and Personal Transformation*. The first function, he writes, is the mystical or metaphysical function, meaning spiritual experiences. The second function is the cosmological function, or painting a coherent, persuasive picture of the universe. The third function is the sociological function, providing laws and customs to live by. And the fourth function is pedagogical, or psychological, offering guidance for how to navigate the journey of life and its many changes.[10] Each of these functions describes a vital way to be centered—spiritually, physically, socially, and psychologically—and myth contains metaphors for all of them.

In teaching this fourfold approach again and again for so many years, Campbell came to embody it. This helped him create the foundation for an enchanted life.

And isn't it interesting that Weber's work focused so heavily on only one of these domains, the sociological? In the passage quoted above, Weber points out that the public sphere—and therefore his own work—neglected "sublime values" such as mysticism, which Campbell defines as the first and most important function of myth: the feeling of "awe and mystery and gratitude for the ultimate mystery of being."[11] Weber seems to have known what he was missing. Further, if mysticism is fundamental to enchantment, as Weber suggests, and is fundamental to mythology, as Campbell insists, then it follows that myth and enchantment have something important to do with each other.

In a related vein, Campbell defines bliss as "that deep sense of being present, of doing what you absolutely must do to be yourself"[12]—in other words, embracing your inner maverick. "Your bliss can guide you to the transcendent mystery," he says, "because bliss is the welling up of the energy of the transcendent wisdom within you."[13] So bliss is wisdom and leads to the enchantment of mysticism, or spiritual experience. If this is true, which I think it is, then the language of mysticism, myth, and bliss can be a vocabulary of enchantment unique to each person, to their particular path, and to their irreplaceable contributions to the world.

## ENCHANTMENT, MYTH, AND BLISS, OH MY

For the purposes of this book, let's define disenchantment as that which is boring, rote, flat, dull, ugly, restrictive, controlled, or any combination of the above.

Enchantment, on the other hand, is that which is marked by Weber's "ultimate and most sublime values," or love and mysticism, together with all their connotations of fun, blessing, luck, charm, beauty, awe, and wonder. For me, enchantment is a way of experiencing the world while leaning into joy, creativity, and possibility.

Myth remains a sparkling avenue into enchantment. Mythic stories and images act as antidotes to Weber's imbalanced intellectualizing, and to day-to-day routines. For one thing, myths activate image-based, metaphorical imagination in addition to verbal literalism. They provide a way to dis-identify with your own experiences by viewing them through mystical, magical, myth-vision goggles as new incarnations of ancient patterns.

When I experience my life as a small manifestation of repeating mythic motifs, I take things less personally. I feel like I'm participating in something beyond myself. I see past the threshold guardians of fear and desire that Campbell talks about[14] and into the charmed garden, a mythic metaphor for the mystery, the unknown and unknowable source of beauty from which the cosmos and I arise. Following myth into the mystery is one way I can practice enchantment.

## IMAGINE, IF YOU WILL

Once, when visiting a cathedral in France, I marveled at all the mundane scenes memorialized in the gorgeous medieval stained-glass windows. Farmers pushed wheelbarrows. Masons cut stone. Smiths forged iron and shoed horses.

"But why on earth," I wondered, "would the artists have labored over such pedestrian images for this sacred space? Why not create angels and saints radiating divine glory?"

Then I realized my mistake: the *point* of windows was the daily grind, because the light of enchantment can shine through anything.

With the MythBlast essays in this book, I tried to write my way to something akin to that same illumination: words rather than glass that let some light shine through. Writing these essays helped me experience imagination, metaphor, beauty, and bliss, and helped me understand more fully that these abstract ideas are renewable resources. I believe they surround us like radio waves of enchantment. The more I tune into them, the more the signal strengthens.

What, you might ask, is a MythBlast essay? It's a genre invented by the Joseph Campbell Foundation, where each week a writer in the myth community explores ideas from Campbell's expansive body of work in the context of some pre-specified monthly theme. Some of the themes you'll see here include books by Joseph Campbell, mythic motifs, and specific images such as individual tarot cards. MythBlasts are brief by design, intended to offer a moment of mythic insight during otherwise hectic schedules. Because of Campbell's enchanted oeuvre, writing them gave me a welcome playground for practicing enchantment.

Each of these essays changed me somehow. Each taught me something and gave me new perspectives and new thoughts. Each served me a dram of enchantment by enabling me to think deeply about myth and the work of Joseph Campbell. Writing about myth helped me make it through some difficult times beginning in 2020, the first year of the Covid-19 pandemic. The healing balm of the creative process was a salve for my stress, and mythic images helped me create distance between me and my worries, between me and my inner Max Weber. The more I recognized mythic patterns at play, the less personal my worries became and the more magical and meaningful they seemed. I felt connected to all the others who had worked through struggles similar to mine, and to all those who would follow.

The myths also gave me a sense of participatory agency, because no myth is ever finished. Myths are always subject to new ideas, new imaginings, new revisions. You can rewrite the next scene, reassign cast members, change the setting, craft entirely new outcomes.

Because what if enchantment suffuses the universe? What if, in some sense, enchantment is what we're made of? What if the imagery of myth suggests exactly that? Wouldn't that constitute the most fun and rewarding call to adventure imaginable? Wouldn't that be a bliss worth following?

## ABOUT THIS BOOK

The Joseph Campbell Foundation enabled me to imagine into these ideas, for which I'll always be grateful. I didn't realize when I was writing that the essays would show up together someday, and yet they do resolve into some clear themes: tricksters, dreams, goddesses, and my family, so those are the sections you'll find here.

Each essay closes with reflection questions and a creative prompt, because I'm a big believer in creativity as a method of practicing enchantment. I hope you'll feel wildly free to adapt these prompts to any and all forms of creative expression: sewing, cooking, painting, writing, sculpting, dancing, singing, woodworking, or whatever your medium might be.

You'll also find what I think of as bliss blurbs, which are my personal reflections about applying Campbell's ideas. If the strategy is *follow your bliss*, then these little blurbs are bliss tactics, so to speak—reminders about getting on and staying on the bliss wagon. But it's important to note that bliss following can get self-centered if it goes too far, and if it isn't grounded in relational values. So, with these bliss blurbs, the invitation is to hold them in an ethic of care, compassion, and respect for all beings.

For me, practicing enchantment offers a way of trying to get into my corner of the metaphorical garden to pull weeds, spread mulch, plant flowers, and invite friends over for a picnic. It's a way to craft the experience of being alive. When life feels shallow, pointless, hopeless, hapless, that's the hardest time to practice enchantment, and that's when it's most important.

Max Weber suffered from an enchantment deficiency, bless his brilliant soul. Joseph Campbell's ideas offer an alternative.

**NOTES**

1  Jason Ā. Josephson-Storm. *The Myth of Disenchantment: Magic, Modernity, and the Birth of the Human Sciences.* U of Chicago P, 2017, 270.

2  Mario Marotta. "A disenchanted world: Max Weber on magic and modernity." *Journal of Classical Sociology.* March 2023, 3. DOI: 10.1177/1468795x231160716.

3  H.H. Gerth and C. Wright Mills. "Introduction." *From Max Weber: Essays in Sociology.* Routledge, 2009, 11.

4  Max Weber. "Science as a Vocation." *From Max Weber: Essays in Sociology,* edited and introduced by H.H. Gerth and C. Wright Mills. Routledge, 2009, 155.

5  Marotta, 1-2.

6  Gerth and Mills, 12.

7  Ibid, 14.

8  Ibid, 11.

9  Stephen and Robin Larsen. *A Fire in the Mind: The Life of Joseph Campbell.* Doubleday, 1991, 84.

10 Joseph Campbell. *Pathways to Bliss: Mythology and Personal Transformation*. New World Library, 2004, 104, 105, 107.

11 Ibid, 104.

12 Ibid, xxiii.

13 Ibid, xxiv.

14 Joseph Campbell, *Thou Art That: Transforming Religious Metaphor*. New World Library, 2001, 51.

# PART I
# Trickster Sightings

# *In the* COMPANY *of* COYOTE

*This essay is about the mythological Trickster by way of an experience I had with literal coyotes. I wrote this MythBlast at a time when my inner fire felt cold and quenched, but the Trickster and Joseph Campbell (who had a fair amount of Trickster himself!) led me to a memory from twenty years earlier that helped relight an inner spark. It seems fitting, too, that this experience happened when I lived in New Mexico. Every time I flew into Albuquerque and took the air-port shuttle bus to the rental car building, a recorded message over the loudspeaker boomed, "Welcome to the land of enchantment!"*

*Originally published on June 26, 2022.*

When I lived on a mesa in northern New Mexico, one summer night I left every window open so the starlit, indigo air could cool the house after a long, hot day. It seemed like I had barely fallen asleep when a shrill, continuous shrieking woke me so fast that I was up and out of bed before my eyes opened all the way. That otherworldly screaming swirled around me like auditory sparks in the gray pre-dawn light. I dashed to the bedroom window.

Outside, not ten feet away, sat a coyote, letting loose with a piercing *kai-yai-yai*, but the sound encircled me, like it came from inside the house as well as the bedroom window. Wide awake now, I raced to the kitchen. Another coyote *kai-yai*-ed outside that window, too. All around the house—north, south, east, west—coyotes had surrounded the walls to voice their spine-tingling cry. So much sound from those small bodies! The song flared on and on through the open windows, filling the rooms from floor to ceiling.

Breathless, I hovered by the back patio door, facing east, to listen and watch the coyote who sat there. One coyote among many, yes, but also Coyote, an archetypal field of energy, a flame of the soul whose flickering, shifting shape can represent a larger pattern often called the Trickster.

In his book *The Masks of God: Primitive Mythology*, Joseph Campbell introduces tricksters from many cultures and eras, as is his way, in traditions that range from Indigeneity to Christianity. Campbell hypothesizes that Trickster was the primary figure of myth in the Paleolithic age, creating the world and bringing fire to the people.[1] Here we can read "world" and "fire" as metaphors for culture, but we can also read them as psychological images. Trickster can return to us our inner flame, the sparks that sometimes sputter out along the way, the embers of personal creativity and world-making.

In New Mexico, I often saw coyotes loping along sidewalks, trails, and suburban lawns, thriving at the edges of human civilization. Wiry bundles of cunning and energy, snouts always pointing toward new possibilities, they ate everything from beetles to garbage to pets.

The Trickster's amorality means they never integrate into society. Instead, they represent the perpetual stranger who exists outside the known order. But isn't it so often the stranger who shakes up moribund routines? Who reminds us to stay alert?

Who ignites new ideas? Stories of Trickster tell of the fires of life as they exist outside established rules, precisely in order to change those rules when necessary. Trickster fires can burn, but they can also turn food into feasts and thaw frozen hearts.

When the coyotes finished their song, they moved away from my east-facing patio. Reunited, the pack paused together in the morning twilight. Now I could see all five of them. One sat down and rested a furry chin on the back of another who was still standing. Together, they gazed across the valley toward the mountains in the distance. They waited. And waited. And then the sun came up over that ridge, right where they were looking. The valley filled with golden light that limned juniper trees and yucca plants and the coyotes' coats with liquid marigold brilliance. Then the coyotes trotted off down the mesa together.

The morning still quivered with their jubilant song. Their placid companionship. Their witnessing presence at the sacred birth of a new dawn, unlike any other that had happened before or would ever happen again. Coyote called that day into being and woke me so we could watch it together.

We are not alone. We are companioned by beings other than humans, by forces that sing and shape our shared experience. Why did Coyote sing so loudly that summer morning? Well, why not? Why not set aside self-doubt and self-consciousness? Why not sing with everything you have and everything you are, as though summoning the sun's fire to earth? Why not create, and then be still, to watch the magic of a new day roll over the horizon?

## REFLECTION QUESTIONS

What metaphorical songs has the Trickster reminded you to sing? How has Trickster helped you sing differently when you needed a change? Are there any areas of your life that could use a Trickster song right now?

## CREATIVE PROMPT: TRICKSTER TUNES

Make a playlist of songs that delight your inner trickster. Keep this playlist to yourself; no one else needs to know about it. Make time and space in your schedule to play these songs and sing along as loudly as you can.

**NOTES**

1   Joseph Campbell. *The Masks of God: Primitive Mythology*. New World Library, 2021, 273-76.

# *The* ANTLERED CHILD:
## CHANGING SHAPES, CHANGING SOULS

*I wrote this MythBlast in the autumn of 2021, when the Covid-19 pandemic had been underway for over a year, with all its death, disease, and social upheaval. I include it with other Trickster essays because shapeshifting is such a trickster skill, and I felt like we were all shapeshifting along with global events. When change is required, the question becomes how to use that change to effect other, adjacent changes. In this case, the changes gave me the opportunity to change by writing about change. Joseph Campbell's book, Creative Mythology, and the mythic imagery of the Netflix series Sweet Tooth combined to help me imagine into and change with the massive changes sweeping the world.*

*Originally published on October 17, 2021.*

Change is in the air. Again. As usual.

The climate is changing. The pandemic changes. Technology changes. Our lives change.

Once upon a time, change happened more gradually, or so it seems. Now it feels like the pace of change has accelerated. I don't seem to have the proper decompression chambers in which to adjust, and more changes are coming whether I choose them or not.

But we still have myth, creativity, and our ability to create new myths, as Joseph Campbell discusses in Volume 4 of his

*Masks of God* series, *Creative Mythology*. Creative myth-making, Campbell says,

> restores to existence the quality of adventure, at once shattering and reintegrating the fixed, already known, in the sacrificial creative fire of the becoming thing that is nothing at all but life, not as it *will be* or *should be*, as it *was* or as it *never will be*, but as it *is*, in depth, in process, *here and now*, inside and out.[1]

In other words, the myths we make give our present-moment lives back to us with the added thrill of adventure. They help us meet and imagine the changes we face.

One example of life-giving creative mythology is *Sweet Tooth* (2021), a Netflix series set in a world where a new animal-human hybrid species evolves at the same time a pandemic sweeps the planet. *Sweet Tooth* happens in a post-TV, post-internet, post-consumer landscape in which the population of humanity has been vastly reduced. But violent remnants of a controlling, dominion-prone, fear-based culture still cling to existence in the form of an army of Last Men who hunt the child hybrids. The show focuses on the adventures of a hybrid named Gus who was born with the body of a human but the ears, antler nubs, and senses of a deer. In other words, Gus embodies what shamans might experience through trance and dance: a joining of human and animal consciousness. Gus grows up in isolation in a remote forested stretch of what used to be Yellowstone National Park. As Gus grows, so do his antlers, and when the time is right, he sets out on an adventure that carries him away from home.

Not far into his travels, a band of Last Men corners Gus inside a former park visitors' center. Little Gus, armed with a homemade slingshot, faces off against a Last Man who carries a high-powered rifle when, in the open doorway behind Gus, a massive buck appears who is clearly there to protect the child. With antlers too wide for the buck to step through the door, his presence is utterly arresting. The Last Man seems paralyzed by the same astonishment we, the viewers,[2] feel at suddenly finding ourselves in the presence of the sublime: powers beyond our own, dimensions of life of which we had been oblivious, more beauty and love than we had thought possible. In that moment, Gus, unaware of the buck, becomes the child of the buck, of the antlered Celtic god Cernunnos,[3] and of the antlered human figure on the wall in the Cave of the Trois-Frères.[4] We feel all those antlers ourselves—their bony anchors in our skulls, the heft of their weight on our necks and backs, the instinctive urge to lower horns and charge. The sacred buck shows us Gus's strength and destiny: simultaneously peaceful and powerful, an herbivore-warrior who will fight for what he loves. Here, the buck overwhelms his opponent simply through the force of his presence.

*Sweet Tooth*'s creative myth-making opens other windows onto the sacred as well. In the first episode, Gus learns that rain is "just Mother Nature, washing herself clean." The show's Animal Army organizes around the belief that hybrids are a miracle of nature. A character named Dr. Singh sees the divine in Gus thanks to a gift that Singh's wife gave him, a statue of a Hindu goddess who once appeared as a deer. As an embodiment of sacred nature, Gus's part-human and part-deer form speaks of the sacred nature of all animals, human and otherwise. In fact, Gus's form affirms that we are sacred *because* of our animal nature, and so is the rest of our extended animal family. Human-animal hybrids remind us that we are animals, and that our souls—our *animas*, to use the Latin term—are animal souls.

The myth-makers of *Sweet Tooth* also suggest that physical shapes and psychological shapes change together, and neither is fixed. Our birthright vitality and consciousness, from which the technological world likes to separate us, remain rooted in the adaptability of our bodies and the organic world. External metamorphosis coincides with internal metamorphosis. What's more, stasis doesn't actually exist. The universe, which includes our Earth and ourselves, is ever and always in froth and flux.

*Sweet Tooth* is a creative myth about creativity, illustrating new ways of being in response to change. I have already been called upon to make many changes in my life. I can rest assured I will need to make more. *Sweet Tooth* says I can, and also suggests how and why. Another clue comes from Campbell, who points out that mythic images "touch and exhilarate centers of life beyond the reach of vocabularies of reason and coercion."[5] I can change creatively and mythically, in order to reclaim and exhilarate my sacred animal life.

## REFLECTION QUESTIONS

What images and ideas do you associate with deer? What might it feel like to have antlers? How would having antlers change how you move through the world?

## CREATIVE PROMPT: YOUR ANIMAL SELF

What's your favorite kind of animal or the first animal that comes to mind? Draw a picture of that animal, or find a drawing of the animal that you can color, or find your favorite image of that animal on the internet. Put the image someplace prominent for a few days, maybe on your phone's lock screen, or on the refrigerator or a bulletin board. Notice if and how your perceptions change when the animal is present in your imagination.

### NOTES

1   Joseph Campbell. *The Masks of God: Creative Mythology*. Penguin, 1968, 7-8.

2   Jim Mickle and Beth Schwartz. *Sweet Tooth*. Season 1, episode 2, "Sorry About All the Dead People," 38:15-41:50.

3   Joseph Campbell, *Creative Mythology*, 412.

4   Joseph Campbell. *The Masks of God: Primitive Mythology*. New World Library, 2021, 284.

5   Joseph Campbell, *Creative Mythology*, 4.

*Follow your bliss*

*means follow your fascinations.*

*What captivates your imagination, draws*

*your attention, sends a sizzle of interest*

*crackling through your soul?*

# The HERO-HEART *in the* CLASSROOM

*As 2023 was drawing to a close, I was preparing to teach a course on a subject I love: folklore and fairy tales. Writing this essay reminded me of the Trickster aspects of teaching, and the Trickster tricks of some of my most beloved and influential teachers, among whom I count Joseph Campbell. Even though I never met him in person, his work led me to my work, and his ideas continue to help me shape my life.*

*Originally published on January 7, 2024.*

I love to hear stories about when people first encountered mythology, or how they first felt themselves drawn to myth. There's often a sense of breathless amazement and detailed recollections that accompany seismic moments like these. For many in the myth community, our mythic origin stories speak to when we first found the work of Joseph Campbell.

My first encounter with Campbell's ideas was in the late 1980s in a college English class called "Introduction to Folklore." I was attending a large, conservative, religious university with strict oversight of course syllabi to make sure we students weren't exposed to anything that might challenge our belief in the literal truth of scripture. Instructors had a Sunday-best dress code—suits and ties for men, skirts or dresses for women—and we all had to sign an honor code promising not only that we would behave ourselves in all the required ways, but that we would inform on any students we saw breaking the rules. I'll never forget that Orwellian sense of living beneath a theocratic tyranny. But the Folklore class met in a small room tucked away at the end of a basement hallway in a quiet evening time slot, and the class had only fifteen or twenty students. It felt like I was able to inhabit a forgotten pocket of freedom away from the glare of religious assessment and evaluation. In an act of rebellion which my younger self found thrilling, the professor wore blue jeans and flannel shirts. One day, in another gesture of defiance, he brought a copy of Joseph Campbell's *The Hero with a Thousand Faces* to class and read out loud to us. I don't remember the passage he read, but I remember the electricity in the air. I felt like I was floating on it.

The second time I encountered Campbell's work was in another English class, this one at a scruffy public community college where I enrolled after leaving the religious university. The class topic was nature writing, and one day the teacher interrupted our normal activities to march us into the media room to watch Episode One of *Joseph Campbell and the Power of Myth with Bill Moyers*, "The Hero's Adventure." Now I could see Campbell and hear his voice out loud.

"My general formula for my students," he said to Bill Moyers from the television screen, "is follow your bliss! I mean, find where it is and don't be afraid to follow it."[1] These words nourished me as I struggled to put my life back together after stepping away from religion. *Hero*, of course, phrases the idea more obliquely: "the hero-heart must be at hand."[2] Where *Hero*'s literary prose is highly crafted, *The Power of Myth* is conversational, but both works illustrate Campbell's signature commitment to the underlying unity of mythic traditions, the diversity of expressions through which the mythic spirit speaks, and the psychological state that lends itself to a life well lived.

In different voices, both works reveal Campbell's insights about heroes, adventure, and bliss. *Hero* discusses bliss more objectively in the context of recurring mythic patterns, and *The Power of Myth* makes it practical: follow your bliss already! The implication, I think, is that following bliss has much to do with living the hero's adventure. It's about saying yes to its invitations, which means heeding what calls to you regardless of what anyone else says, because the alternative would shrink your soul and leave you filled with regret. Following bliss means facing fear head on and daring to see through it, past it, to the possibilities that await on the other side. It means rebellion and defiance. It means summoning your hero-heart's reserves of courage.

Heroism and bliss-following are lived soul experiences, psychological states marked by a willingness to risk danger on behalf of someone or something you believe in—very much like my professor who defied university rules to read Campbell to us. He put himself in real jeopardy. At that same school, I saw a group of young, muscular, angry zealots confront a beleaguered biology professor because he had dared to teach evolution. If anyone in the Folklore class had reported the professor, he could easily have faced personal, professional, and religious retribution. But he had the courage to defy a system that was trying to control and contain him and us. By bringing *Hero* to that basement classroom, he brought heroism as well, in word and deed. By reading to us about heroes, he showed us what it meant to be one.

Campbell died before I took either of those English classes, so in a sense he was speaking to me from beyond the veil, as he still does today through works like *Hero* and *The Power of Myth*. When my professor read to us from *Hero* the book had already been inspiring readers for almost forty years. The year 2024 marks the seventy-fifth anniversary of its publication, and the book gives every indication of still going strong, with its unique combination of insight, awe, and wisdom.

Neither of my teachers made Campbell a homework assignment. Neither put him on the syllabus or in any kind of test. They just saw to it that he joined us in the classroom. In so doing, they each embraced the radical, subversive heroism of educating our hearts, souls, and imaginations as well as our minds. I am forever grateful to both of them.

## REFLECTION QUESTIONS

Who have been your most important teachers? To whom have you taught important lessons? If you could learn one thing today, anything at all, what would it be?

## CREATIVE PROMPT: YOUR HEROIC TEACHER HEART

Prepare a lesson plan to teach yourself something you know you need to learn. Include readings, homework assignments, lecture topics, assessments, and a final project.

## NOTES

1 Joseph Campbell. "Episode One: The Hero's Adventure." *Joseph Campbell and the Power of Myth with Bill Moyers.* Apostrophe S Productions, Inc. in association with Alvin H. Perlmutter, Inc., Public Affairs Television, Inc., 1988, 40:30-40:45.

2 Joseph Campbell. *The Hero with a Thousand Faces.* New World Library, 2008, 18.

# Returning *to the* World

*In the fall of 2023 I spent some time in London, writing, visiting museums, and eating food from around the world. I was amazed all over again, as I am every time I travel, at how refreshing it is to change the scenery, to change the sensations of life. These experiences are some of the many gifts of the Trickster, who is most at home on the open road. Writing this essay on the plane ride back to the United States, inspired by The Inner Reaches of Outer Space by Joseph Campbell and the Fool tarot card, I felt like the experience of travel coalesced in my memory in a deeper way than simply journaling it or talking about it would have done.*

*Originally published on December 17, 2023.*

I'm sitting in the middle seat on an airplane flying west over the Atlantic Ocean. My tray table holds a flimsy cup of strong coffee, a pen, a pad, and a book, *The Inner Reaches of Outer Space: Metaphor as Myth and as Religion* by Joseph Campbell. The chairs beside me are occupied, so my elbows remain tucked in against my sides. Only my hands and forearms can move as I gingerly raise and lower the coffee, steady the pad to write, or hold the book up to read.

*Inner Reaches* is one of my favorite Campbell books, with its focus on imagination and art. I love the title, too, suggesting the infinite inwardness of the cosmos, and the cosmic reaches of the inner self. I'm reading Campbell's reflections on NASA's photo of earth from the moon, an image which "lacks those lines of sociopolitical divisions that are so prominent on maps,"[1] when I glance up from the book and notice that the screen on the seat in front of me shows an animation of the airplane's path as though from above. Not as far away as the moon, but high enough to see the planet's curve and the contours of continents.

At intervals, this image of the globe spins on its virtual axis, a gratuitous pirouette for no purpose other than to entertain us passengers. Some places are labeled, but the graphic shows no borders. There go Canada and the United States, the Pacific Ocean, Japan, Mongolia, Turkey, Norway, Spain. It's nighttime over Tokyo, Hong Kong, Delhi, Dubai. In the animation, cities necklace the land with yellow beads of electric light.

Campbell believed the image of the world from space might bring humanity together and usher in a new myth, a "mythology of this unified earth as of one harmonious being."[2] The key word here is "being," an entity possessed of animate wholeness, like a person is. And because beings in myth are so often imagined as goddesses and gods, Campbell could be wondering how a new myth might emerge of Earth as sacred, honored, and archetypal, a deity to be met in heart-space with reverence and awe. But to see a being in a photo of a planet requires mythic images and mythic imagination.

Which brings us to the tarot cards. In the tarot deck's image-rich major arcana, the last card is the World, number twenty-one. If the Fool begins the cards' metaphorical journey, the World completes the adventure. In some decks, the World shows a nearly nude figure adorned only with a sportive scarf that floats in undulating waves like Aphrodite's magical, love-inducing wrap. Fully formed and fully breasted, the person is an adult, not a child. This figure's beauty is vibrantly alive, suggesting metaphorically the living, loving soul of a living, loving world. Hovering in clouds at the corners of the card are other beings: angel, eagle, lion, bull. The four of them surround the World, who holds a magic wand in each hand as lightly as though about to twirl them. A powerful, ensouled being supported by other powerful souls, the World works magic effortlessly, with both hands at once.

I'm flying to New York after a few weeks in London, where I saw thrilling art and architecture, savored global food and wine, and walked among throngs of people from everywhere who spoke more languages than I could identify. My visit felt like an encounter with the world up close and personal: a fountain of life, a ferment of making, a fertile tumult of blending and re-blending. The creativity of the city seemed spontaneously buoyant, and now I feel replenished with insights and experiences. This radically different vantage point gave my day-to-day world an infusion of fresh perspectives, the way the Earthrise photo gave us all a new view of our shared home.

The tarot card's metaphorical World dances through a massive wreath. It's an opening bound by an eternal circle, hence an opening into eternity, or a space outside time. The World hovers between realities, suspended between everything that came before and everything yet to come. This card of culmination shows the fleeting, floating simultaneity of endings and beginnings and the infinite expanse between. The World's immense, generous love creates beauty in those transitions as if by magic.

My coffee is almost gone. The plane approaches New York. When I finally stretch my folded limbs and exit the aircraft, stepping out of the oval doorway I entered only a few hours ago, I will hover for a heartbeat in a timeless space of possibility before returning to the world from my brief time away. I will cross the plane's threshold a different person than when the flight began, different than when I left home. After passing through that portal, I will step into the realm of the Fool again, because when one journey ends another begins. I hope for some of the Fool's radiant faith, relaxed in the gnosis of what it is that waits at the end of the next adventure.

Or rather, who it is who waits.


## REFLECTION QUESTIONS

In what ways do you experience any part of the world as a living being? In what ways do you experience the whole world as a living being? In what ways do you experience yourself as a microcosmic version of the world or of any part of it?

## CREATIVE PROMPT: YOUR PLANETARY SELF

Let's say the world is a living being with a loving soul. Let's say everything you normally think of as inert matter actually pulsates with vibrant energy. Let's say that same energy pulses through you, so when you speak or write or paint or sculpt, you give expression to that soul. How might this possibility affect one thing you speak or write or paint or sculpt today?

**NOTES**

1 Joseph Campbell. *The Inner Reaches of Outer Space: Metaphor as Myth and as Religion.* New World Library, 2002, 94.

2 Ibid, xix.

# PART 2
# Myth and Dreams

# DREAMING *the* LOTUS

*In 2019, I completed my graduate work in mythological studies and defended my dissertation—just in time for a pandemic to sweep the world. Luckily, miraculously, blissfully, I connected with the Joseph Campbell Foundation right before the nation shut down in 2020. While I was working on the team that would eventually publish the Foundation's Skeleton Key Study Guides, I was invited to contribute an essay to the MythBlast series. This is my first MythBlast, inspired by Campbell's book Asian Journals and my dissertation's focus on creation myth and creativity.*

*Originally published on August 2, 2020.*

Joseph Campbell's book *Asian Journals* includes an essay called "Hinduism," in which Campbell shares a mythological overview of this ancient Indian religious tradition. In one Hindu creation myth that he describes, the god Viṣṇu sleeps on the back of a great serpent named Ananta, or Endless, who floats on the waves of a primordial sea.[1] According to a medieval version of the myth, during Viṣṇu's divine rest "there arose in play from his navel a pure lotus, wondrous and divine.... Spreading out 100 leagues, bright as the morning sun, it had a heavenly fragrance."[2] This is the brilliant, playful, perfumed flower upon which the creator Brahmā will meditate before making the world.

David R. Kinsley sees this lotus as an "effortless reflex of a god who creates the entire universe while asleep; he dreams the universe into existence."[3] So Viṣṇu's creativity requires no efforting, as we say these days. It only needs REM sleep, or the complete opposite of work. Others see the lotus as "a masculine image of bodily reproduction,"[4] and truly, Brahmā does emerge from this lotus and its umbilical stem. But the scholar of gender and religion June Campbell (no relation to Joseph) cites Joseph Campbell's observation that the lotus represents the goddess Padma, whose name means "lotus" and whose body is the universe: Because umbilical energy flows from the mother to the child's navel, this maternal lotus must be nourishing Viṣṇu, not the other way around.[5] I think the lotus gracefully holds both views. Dreamer and dream effortlessly sustain each other. In a sense, they create each other, because without the dreamer, there is no dream, and without his dream, Viṣṇu could not be a dreamer.

The lotus also illustrates the gifts of dreams. Creative people in just about every sphere of endeavor report new ideas and creative breakthroughs in the content of their dreams, and the culture of India is particularly comfortable with the possibility of goddesses and gods sending guidance through dreams. The lotus rising from Viṣṇu's navel, the navel representing the core of his being, is a mythological example of a creative idea that arrives in a dream, with a feeling of miracle, magic, and divine grace. The lotus is an image of an inspired dream.

Joseph Campbell sees Viṣṇu, the serpent, and the ocean as three expressions of the same "subtle substance that the wind of the mind stirs into action," giving rise to the dream of the world.[6] Campbell continues, "just as, in your dreams, all the images that you behold and all the people who appear are really manifestations of your own dreaming power, so are we all manifestations of Viṣṇu's dreaming power.... Hence, we are all one in Viṣṇu: manifestations, inflections, of this dreaming power."[7] In other words, we might seem to be separate, but actually you, I, and the universal lotus are all the same. We are divine creativity.

Campbell's creative approach to myth is on full display in these passages. He practiced a form of mythopoesis, except that instead of expressing myths themselves poetically, in the way of the *Odyssey* for example, he writes poetically *about* myth. His poetic mythologizing, meaning his poetic study of myth, was attuned to metaphor, meaning, beauty, and wonder. In *Asian Journals*, Campbell himself reflects on what he sees as two primary positions in the Hindu tradition: one that focuses on unchangeable truths, and another position that "harken[s] to the voice of the living God, the Muse."[8] I can practically see him leaning in to receive that divine inspiration in order to write about divine inspiration. He goes on: "I tend, therefore, to associate the work of the creative genius in art, literature, science and mathematics with the living, creative aspect of my subject,"[9] meaning he associates creativity with myth. He was a creative mythologist and a mythological creator. His mythological creativity inspires me to build on his work through my own.

Dreams arrive in our consciousness in much the same way as creative breakthroughs: like surprise guests bearing gifts. Myths, too, come into being through creativity. Myth and dream arise from the same source, the same font of imagination from which all creativity flows.

Viṣṇu always reclines on the muscular coils of the eternal serpent, rocking on the waves of the cosmic sea. The fragrant lotus blossoms on, lighting up that mythic landscape, sustaining Viṣṇu and supporting Brahmā. Creator goddesses and gods represent creativity each in their own way, but they all remind us that creativity is sacred, and the sacred is creative.

## REFLECTION QUESTIONS

If Viṣṇu dreams a world dream, and Campbell dreams a myth dream, what dream arises from the core of your being? What lotus creates and feeds your inner Viṣṇu?

## CREATIVE PROMPT: DREAM JOURNAL

By writing down your dreams first thing in the morning, keep a dream journal for one week, or as long as it takes to record images from a handful of dreams. From each dream, choose a single image or idea, and then combine all those images into one new creative project in any medium you like: dance, textiles, carpentry, writing, song, or any other art form.

**NOTES**

1  Joseph Campbell. *Asian Journals.* New World Library, 2002, 314.

2  Cornelia Dimmitt and J.A.B. van Buitenen. *Classical Hindu Mythology: A Reader in the Sanskrit Purāṇas*, Temple UP, 1978, 30

3  David R. Kinsley. *The Divine Player: A Study of Kṛṣṇa Līlā.* Motilal Banarsidass, 1979, 2.

4  Dimmit and van Buitenen, 17.

5  June Campbell. *Traveller in Space: Gender, Identity and Tibetan*

*Buddhism.* Continuum, 2002, 58.

6  Joseph Campbell, *Asian Journals*, 314.

7  Ibid, 314.

8  Ibid, 176.

9  Ibid, 176.

***Follow your bliss***
*means follow your favorites.*
*Choose little things you love*
*and they'll lead to more things you love*
*until one day you look up and you're in a bliss field*
*you could never have dreamed up on your own.*

# Releasing *the* Dreamings

*When I was young, my friends called me JoJo. Later, when I was preparing to begin graduate work in mythological studies, I joked that the degree would turn me into JoJo Campbell. Obviously that didn't happen, but I certainly learned more about Joseph Campbell, not least through volunteering in the archives that held some of his photos. It was an incredible experience of what felt like a true encounter with someone whose ideas inspire me so profoundly.*

*Originally published on July 3, 2022.*

When I was in graduate school studying mythology, I volunteered in the archives that housed Joseph Campbell's papers. My job was to create high-resolution scans of Campbell's personal photos—baby pictures, childhood, youth, adulthood, snapshots from his later years. Sitting at a computer workstation in that windowless basement office, I carefully positioned each piece of paper on the glass face of the scanner, clicked the Scan button, then zoomed way in on the digital file to make sure to capture clean edges of the original. I often found myself staring at those close-up images, captivated by the eyes of the people in the scenes. My impression of Campbell himself changed as I worked. He became less of a disembodied voice on the page, and more of a real, actual person who seemed to have lived intensely and intentionally.

Campbell's book, *Correspondence: 1927–1987,* includes a letter he wrote to the artist Angela Gregory in 1928, when he was twenty-four years old. He writes:

> I know that the constant drumming of things around one can upset the pulse of one's heart. But after all it's inside our own hearts that beauty reposes. Pleasures and pains affect the body; and if our dreamings have never released our souls, then pleasures and pains will upset our mental and emotional tranquility. Aggravations and disappointments—and even a certain blankness can help the soul to grow in understanding, once the soul has learned to feed upon whatever comes its way.[1]

I can picture the passion in his young face as he composed these words. I can hear the urgency that would drive his voice if he were to speak them out loud. *If our dreamings have never released our souls*—he's talking about loosening the tendency to over-identify with the trappings of life, of religion and belief systems, desires, political ideas, relationships, and even our bodies, and mistake them for who we really are. The alternative to letting those dreamings hold the soul captive, he suggests, is to release our souls not *from* our ideas about life, but from *confusing* them with our ideas about life, to grant the soul freedom to observe experiences the same way Campbell demonstrates how to observe myth—staying alert for truth and beauty.

Further down the page he completes the thought: "When we shall have lived this intensely we should have truth in our hearts and beauty—then our work will be great because we shall be great ourselves."[2]

Living intensely. Living wide awake, with a soul free and released. These are aspirational ideas, no doubt, but Campbell seems to have done a good job of it, releasing his soul from identification with his dreamings, living intensely in the direction of truth and beauty, doing great work. This is one of the boons that Campbell found on the journey of his own life, and he brought it back to share with his community: not only his work itself, but also his *way* of working. He showed that aspirations like these are within reach.

This individual boon also opens the possibility of communities that support their members living intensely and doing great work. For what is a community if not an aggregate of individuals, and what is an individual if not a representative of their community? The souls of individuals affect the community, and the soul of the community affects individuals. This dialectic is fundamental to creative work. Creative people like Joseph Campbell and Angela Gregory continually move back and forth between their communities and their individual imaginations to generate images and ideas, bring them into being, and share them. I see this pattern play out again and again in the community of mythologists—a community that owes so much to Campbell's contributions.

So perhaps I might be permitted to imagine a revision of Campbell's reflections to Angela Gregory, this time as a message to his extended community:

*I know that the constant drumming of things around us can upset the pulse of our hearts. But after all it's inside our own hearts that beauty reposes. Pleasures and pains affect us all; and if our collective dreamings have never released our community's soul, then pleasures and pains will upset the community's mental*

*and emotional tranquility. Aggravations and disappointments—
and even a certain blankness can help the community's soul to
grow in understanding....*

*When the community shall have lived this intensely, the com-
munity will have truth in its heart and beauty—then our work
will be great because we shall be great.*

And isn't myth itself intense? Its outsized imagery, its larger-than-life deities and heroes, its clashings and collaborations
among characters who represent the great powers of Earth and
cosmos? Myths are collective dreamings of Earth's human
communities, and so they represent a perfect practice ground
for zooming in on their images and ideas, freeing the soul from
identifying with those ideas, and thereby cultivating truth and
beauty in our own creative hearts.

## REFLECTION QUESTIONS

How might a community release its soul from false beliefs,
disidentifying from myths that cause misery and harm? How
might a community enter more fully into the realm of truth,
beauty, and creativity? How might a community support its
members in doing the same, each in their own unique way?

## CREATIVE PROMPT: LISTENING FOR WISDOM

Find the highest resolution photo you can of someone whose
work means a lot to you. Zoom in and look straight into their
eyes. Really look. Now listen. Really listen. Now set a timer for
ten minutes and write without stopping or editing about what

that person would tell you if they could speak to you right now. Stop writing when the timer rings, then go back and look over what you wrote. Circle anything that seems especially important.

## NOTES

1 Joseph Campbell. *Correspondence: 1927 – 1987.* New World Library, 2019, 13.

2  Ibid, 13.

# As Beatrice *to* Dante

*This essay is about a dream-like experience that I never shared with anyone until I wrote about it for the MythBlast series. It would have been too weird, too embarrassing, too wild to speak it out loud in anything resembling normal conversation, but the work of Joseph Campbell and the Wheel of Fortune tarot card created a mythic container that could honor this story's truth.*

*Originally published on June 11, 2023.*

One day, long ago, the ever-spinning Wheel of Fortune found me sitting at a desk in an open office workspace, my back to a room full of coworkers. Absorbed in a document on my computer, I had just reached an impasse and needed to go ask someone a question. But at that moment a colleague I hadn't seen for years was striding toward me. He whooshed into the chair beside my desk at the same instant that I whirled around to stand up.

*Whoosh-whirl*—and our faces were way too close together, so close that his leather-and-sandalwood cologne must have mixed up with my jasmine perfume, and I found myself staring deep into unknown eyes without even seeing the rest of this person's face.

But I didn't see his eyes, not really. I saw through them, past them, beyond them into a midnight-blue cosmos where stars explode and nebulae roil with galactic lightning. The whole idea of eyes fell away. I felt like I saw the million invisible dimensions of a soul, its shimmers and flickers spiraling into indigo infinity.

"Hello!" he said.

I jerked back to a decorous distance, stammering, confused. This was a person. A literal, rational, breathing human. And we were at work. I couldn't burst out with an "Oh my goodness, I saw your soul and it's gorgeous!!"

Instead, I stuck to convention. "Hello!"

We chatted and caught up, but a part of my awareness remained drunk with awe, high on the vapors of beauty and magnificence. That feeling of altered consciousness lingered for days as I went through the motions of meetings and emails while the Wheel of Fortune kept turning.

That's the Wheel's job, after all. It turns, turns, turns, turns. In the tarot deck, the Wheel of Fortune depicts the ongoing roll of the universe.

If I didn't know better, I might think this card was a four of something. Four lines forming a compass decorated with four Latin letters, four alchemical sigils, and four Hebrew letters that would spell the name of God if they were all together. In the four corners of the card, four golden animal powers hover on muscular, beating golden wings in four separate clouds while perusing four books.

But the card shows important threes, too: three concentric circles around which three cosmic powers ride like a merry-go-round of Egyptian myth. Apopis, the troublemaking serpent, wiggles down into the thick of things. Anubis, the guide of souls, cruises upward and glances outward as though to say, "Buckle up, kiddos, we're going around again." And a wise, regal Queen Sphinx rules over it all from the top of the Wheel, unperturbed and unperturbable.

Of all the beings on this card, there isn't a single earth-bound human. We see gods, forces, symbols, and ideas, but not one mortal. Instead, powers gather here to show the dynamic processes of the cosmos in a productive, creative tension that keeps the wheel turning.

At any moment, the card says, big things could happen.

But the card shows something else too, something tiny and yet key to the whole image. When I draw a line from the upper left corner to the lower right corner, and then another line from the upper right to the lower left, those lines intersect in the center of the card. What do we find there? The center of the Wheel. The hub. The unmoving spot without which the wheel couldn't turn. This is the stillness required for change, the stillness necessary for new life.

"The New Life," Joseph Campbell observes in *Mythic Worlds, Modern Words: On the Art of James Joyce*, "is the life of the awakened spiritual, poetic ... relationship to the world through the physical realm."[1] Campbell is referring to Dante's *Vita Nuova* and James Joyce's *Portrait of the Artist as a Young Man*, both of which blossom forth from an experience of what we might call the center of the Wheel, where new life emerges from a revelatory moment of awe. That's where Dante stood when he saw Beatrice, where Stephen Daedalus stood when he saw the young woman at the beach, where I stood, so to speak, that day at the office when I saw the cosmos in a colleague's eyes. Campbell calls this experience "a ray of the light of eternity."[2] Once in a while, we inhabit the hub and feel reborn. For Dante and Joyce, the experience inspired singular literature.

"Time and space are gone in the enchantment of the heart," Campbell continues, and I think he's right. The Wheel of Fortune's compass can guide us through the vicissitudes, but the card's center is the aperture to magic.

I never told my coworker what happened that day. But I kept an eye on him for a while, in case he turned inside out in a cloud of purple smoke and revealed to everyone the secret that in the center, you fall in love with everything, anything, and most of all with love itself.

## REFLECTION QUESTIONS

When have you been Dante to someone else's Beatrice? When have you been Beatrice to someone else's Dante? How might either of these experiences change the way you live your life?

## CREATIVE PROMPT:
## FROM THE EDGE TO THE CENTER

Think of a time when you experienced an awakening to your "center," whatever that means to you. Using only abstract forms and as many colors as possible, draw or paint what that experience felt like, perhaps as a sequence of panels like a comic book but with no words.

### NOTES
1 Joseph Campbell. *Mythic Worlds, Modern Words: On the Art of James Joyce.* New World Library, 2016, 35.

2 Ibid, 19.

# PART 3
# Goddess Glories

# SKYWOMAN'S SACRED CREATIVE POWER

*My family comes from beautiful land in what is now New York State where the Haudenosaunee people once lived. The matrilineal Haudenosaunee culture distributes authority and responsibilities among the people in ways that inspired the checks and balances in the United States Constitution, although I wish the Founding Fathers had let themselves be more inspired by Haudenosaunee respect for the intelligence and value of women and the natural world.*

*Originally published on August 21, 2022.*

Recently I had an appointment with a dental hygienist I'd never met before. Making small talk, he asked me what I do. I told him I'm a mythologist, which means I study stories that have meant a lot to a lot of people. Sacred stories. He thought that over for a few minutes, then asked if I focused on any particular myths. Yes, I said, I focus on creation myths.

"Oh yeah," he said. "Genesis."

"That's one of them. But there are lots of others too, from all over the world."

He blinked a few times, then he blurted, "But they all start with the man, right?"

If you've had the good luck to read Robin Wall Kimmerer's book *Braiding Sweetgrass*, you might recall the story she shares about Skywoman.[1] This creation story was and remains sacred to the Haudenosaunee (formerly called Iroquois) alliance of Indigenous nations of the forested hills and lake country in what we now call upstate New York, and other Indigenous people around the Great Lakes. John C. Mohawk's book *Iroquois Creation Story* also tells of the divine creator Skywoman, beginning in Sky World, where she falls through a hole in the ground above, then keeps falling, down through the chasm between that world and this one.

> As her body was sinking through the darkness she saw Fire Dragon (Comet) and he seized her body in flight.... "I will aid you as best as I can in all things so that you can survive when you arrive below."[2]

Fire Dragon accompanies Skywoman a little longer, and then he leaves. She keeps plummeting through the air toward an unlit sea where primordial water-bird beings live, who rush upward to lower her down on their wings. But where will they put this surprising new arrival? There's no land in the world below, only water.

> "Something must be done," said Loon, "to keep her body from sinking." Then Hanoghye (Muskrat) said, "I will dive to the bottom of the water to bring earth for her. It is well known to us that she has creative power and can use this earth."[3]

*It is well known*, the myth says, *that she has creative power.* The ensouled world recognizes in Skywoman a being of great creativity whose medium is earth itself. Soon after this, she creates the land (with the help of Turtle and Muskrat) and gives birth to a divine baby girl.

Reading this story, I feel a jolt of adrenaline when Skywoman falls into the void. Surely she'll die! But she doesn't. The chasm turns out to be neither empty nor lifeless. Helpful, intelligent beings inhabit that space, an indication that the emptiness holds consciousness. The awe-inspiring Fire Dragon—fast, hot, ferocious—swoops in to assist. Bird beings empathize with her and slow her descent. In mythic terms, the void is actually alive and supportive. This scene offers an example of what Joseph Campbell calls "magical aid" which helps Skywoman discover a pervading "benign power" that supports her.[4] And Skywoman's creativity seems to require this separation between realms, to require crossing it. Her difficult downward passage leads her to her deeper work.

Skywoman is an Indigenous creator god, illustrating the creativity of Indigenous cultures and ideas. Skywoman partners with other beings, and her collaborative, ecological creativity arises from an interconnected web. She is a woman, which means she is an example of women's creativity. Not coincidentally, Haudenosaunee nations lived in a matrilineal democracy where women and men both led—a system of government that inspired the founders of the United States. In short, Skywoman is a sacred being in the form of an Indigenous woman who collaborates with the natural world to create a stable, bountiful, beautiful biosphere and society.

What's missing from this story? For one thing, there's no commandment to exercise dominion over other beings. And instead of imagining women as an afterthought who exist for men's pleasure and companionship, Skywoman is a powerful creator in her own right.

The dental hygienist and I went on to have an interesting conversation about science, knowledge, and the limits of scientific knowledge. He was obviously no biblical literalist, and yet he offered a clear example of outdated mythic assumptions at work in the world. Thanks to the Genesis creation story, he believed that he and others of his gender were inherently privileged and entitled to come first.

Myths are stories that have meant a lot to a lot of people. In other words, myths hold great meaning. But meaning by itself has no moral valence or value. It is our job to bring conscious awareness to the many levels of meaning that myths carry—both at the surface and their deeper, more hidden, metaphorical values and assumptions.

I believe this is one of the most important reasons to study sacred stories: to identify values and assumptions that might otherwise go unnoticed. Some values and assumptions are helpful. Some are harmful. It's worthwhile to listen—respectfully, reverently, and with gratitude—to the values and assumptions that divine creators like Skywoman share through their sacred stories.

## REFLECTION QUESTIONS

When have you felt like Skywoman falling through the void? When did everything suddenly change for you? What unexpected helpers came to your aid?

## CREATIVE PROMPT:
## EXPERIENCE SKYWOMAN'S STORY

Watch the video version of Skywoman's myth called *The Iroquois Creation Story*, which is available to stream at the website of the Seneca Art and Culture Center at the Ganondagan Historic Site: ganondagan.org/iroquois-creation-story-film

Create space for this myth to speak to you, and space in your heart to hear.

## NOTES

1  Robin Wall Kimmerer. *Braiding Sweetgrass: Indigenous Wisdom, Scientific Knowledge, and the Teachings of Plants.* Milkweed, 2013, 3-10.

2  John C. Mohawk. *Iroquois Creation Story: John Arthur Gibson and J.N.B. Hewitt's Myth of the Earth Grasper.* Mohawk Publications, 2005, 11.

3  Ibid, 12.

4  Joseph Campbell. *A Joseph Campbell Companion: Reflections on the Art of Living.* Harper Perennial, 1995, 75.

# EVERY BLOOM *a* BLESSING

*The last party I attended before the pandemic closed everything was my own wedding, and what a party it was. But less than a year later, while the world was still shut down, my new husband was diagnosed with cancer. That was a difficult time, but one of the things that got me through was myth. This MythBlast isn't directly about what was going on in my life—at the time I couldn't have written about it if I'd tried—but when I read these pages now, I hear my cry for mythic help between every line, and I feel the blessing of the goddess I was calling to.*

*Originally published on April 4, 2021.*

Once, a very long time ago, the Buddha preached a sermon to his followers by saying nothing at all. Instead of speaking, he held up a single flower. Only one listener, a monk named Mahākāśyapa, heard what that flower had to say and "smiled with joy."[1] Everyone else seems to have missed the point of what has come to be called the Flower Sermon, no doubt returning to their chores and meditation with some chagrin. Because, come on—a flower? What could Mahākāśyapa possibly have seen in a single blossom? Or heard? Or... whatever?

The question is still worth asking today. One possibility is that he perceived something related to the intricate Buddhist teaching of the Flower Garland, or Flower Wreath, which

Campbell summarizes succinctly: "one is all and all are one."[2] In other words, we are inseparable from each other, and I do mean "we" in the broadest possible sense. The Flower Garland goes far beyond the platitude, "we are all connected." This teaching asserts that we all arise from and remain one with a single, indivisible continuity. All existence—meaning all energy, all matter, all beings, all consciousness—is defined by inseparability, which is another way of saying we are defined by our unity, and there is no such thing as a separate self. In other words, "I" don't exist without "you," and neither of "us" exists without the All that gives rise to our experience of illusory and temporary separateness. Beneath what we normally think of as our "selves" exists the vibrant, continuous All, an energy field that imagines us up the same way it imagines up a flower out of stems, leaves, seeds, soil, and all the lives that fed that churning loam throughout the ages, leading up to that singe bloom.

In other words, maybe Mahākāśyapa saw an archetypal Blossom representing the larger-than-life "force that through the green fuse drives the flower," as the poet Dylan Thomas calls it.[3] Maybe the Buddha's flower became transparent to the divine Flowering that moves through us all, that power beyond our own that can make us smile no matter what. That Smile, like Mahākāśyapa's, brings us directly to the lotus throne of the goddess who Campbell calls "the most prominent single figure in the ornamentation of all the early Buddhist monuments"[4]— Lakśmi, whose imagery of beauty and wealth overflows with lotus flowers. Lakśmi is, in effect, the great Bloom. She is the soul of the lotus, the love of blooming, the ability to blossom. She brightens, lightens, en-lightens. She is the consciousness of flowering, and she is the flowering of consciousness. Lakśmi *is* the flowers that fountain around her. She is the profligate abundance of the universe, dispensing glories of many kinds. Hearkening back to the teaching of the Flower Garland, Lakśmi reminds us of our own lotus-essence, because if we really are all one, then our consciousness is inseparable from hers. When the Buddha held her aloft for all to see, she smiled directly into and through Mahākāśyapa.

Beyond religious teachings and mythic images, isn't every bloom a blessing in and of itself? A flower is a gift, a grace, a healing. A blossom is an epiphanic reminder of beauty's inevitability. Simultaneously tiny and profound, each flower holds a revelation. Before that flower, its blossom was impossible to imagine. But when those petals unfurled, the world changed. Where there had been nothing, now exists a rose, or an orchid, or a lotus, or new hope. Maybe Mahākāśyapa marveled: how could this miracle exist? And yet it so manifestly *is*, how could it not exist? The flower's presence could have opened his heart by collapsing the binaries of being and non-being, reminding him of his own miraculous presence and the presence of all things.

Flowers tend to appear in the moments when our hearts are most full: first dates, apologies, weddings, hospital rooms, springtime. Flowers might not speak, but they most certainly proclaim. They herald spring's return to a frozen landscape, peace to the battlefield, beauty to bleakness, healing to illness and injury. Flowers trumpet the news of the soul's open heart—the world's open heart—and the open heart of the cosmos itself. A single flower changed Mahākāśyapa's consciousness, then the consciousness of the entire tradition of Buddhism and therefore the world. Like Lakśmi, his flower consciousness blossomed out of the mud and into the flamboyant generosity of nectar and fragrance that draws pollinators from miles around, and like Lakśmi's, his smile became the truth of beauty and the beauty of truth.

## REFLECTION QUESTIONS

When have you experienced the power of flowers to communicate beyond words? When have they spoken for you, or to you, or both? What were some of the messages they carried?

## CREATIVE PROMPT: FLOWER POWER

Visit a garden or farmer's market or florist shop to soak up the presence of flowers. Then use some nonverbal form of creativity to create a flower: draw, paint, quilt, sculpt, dance, sing a wordless song, make a series of photographs. For extra credit, plant and care for a flower or flowers somewhere around where you live.

## NOTES

1 Joseph Campbell. *The Masks of God: Oriental Mythology*. New World Library, 2021, 421.

2 Ibid, 472.

3 Dylan Thomas. "The force that through the green fuse drives the flower." poets.org/poem/force-through-green-fuse-drives-flower/.

4 Campbell, *Oriental Mythology*, 286.

*Follow your bliss*
means open your heart so you can hear
what it has to say and so you can hear
the hearts of others.

# *To the* FEMALE GOD *of the* LABYRINTH

*This essay is about the most helpful myth I've ever experienced: the story of Ariadne, Theseus, the Minotaur, and the labyrinth. This myth gifted me with images that helped me cope when my former husband was diagnosed with brain cancer. I'll never be able to express fully my gratitude to Ariadne for guiding me then.*

*Originally published on August 29, 2021.*

"And my understanding of the mythological mode is that deities and even people are to be understood in this sense, as metaphors. It's a poetic understanding."
—JOSEPH CAMPBELL[1]

It's the middle of winter. Bedtime. I hear a thump in the bedroom. I go in to find out what happened. My husband is lying in bed on his back, limbs rigid and shaking, jaw working, his unblinking gaze staring straight up. In the direct light from the ceiling, his wide-open eyes are fathomless emeralds, an endless green that I've never seen before. A rush of adrenaline turns my vision crisp and clear as I dial 911—fire trucks and an ambulance fill the street—pulsing red lights in the dark—EMTs come inside and administer seizure medication—they carry him out on a canvas stretcher.

Thousands of years ago, in the labyrinthine caves of southern France, artists drew galleries of stylized horned bulls, majestic and fearsome. The Chauvet Cave has one figure with a man's body and a bull's head, arranged so that this early Minotaur overlaps and wraps another image, this one of a woman's pubic triangle and upper legs. The artist had to have worked by firelight—the smell of smoke, a flickering honey-colored glow, hands brushing the rough stone as images sprang into being where before there had been only blank rock.

It's the day after my husband's seizure. The doctors perform emergency surgery. They cross the threshold of his skull, venture into the cave of his brain, and try to release the pressure caused by a mass that appears on the MRI as a blurry zone without clear edges.

Around 1400 BCE, on the island of Crete, in a civilization whose bull art dazzles us to this day, a clerk recorded an offering of honey to someone whose name is often translated as The Lady of the Labyrinth. Literally translated, however, her name would be "The Female God of the Labyrinth Who Has Great Power."[2] Centuries later mainland Greeks told a story of their hero Theseus, who sailed to Crete to kill a Minotaur who lived at the center of a labyrinth to end the human sacrifice the monster demands. But Theseus could only succeed with the help of Ariadne, whose name means Most Holy.[3] Ariadne gave Theseus a sacred sword with which to kill the Minotaur and a divine ball of thread to lead the way back out of the labyrinth.

Three weeks after surgery. We sit in the surgeon's office with more MRI scans. The mass is cancer, the doctor says. A brain tumor. My husband needs more surgery, this time at a specialist center. This time doctors will go in ready to confront the entity inside.

The Cretan Minotaur was named Asterios, which means Starry One, from the root *astro,* or star.[4] So Asterios was a brilliant but dangerous being, an animate, cannibalistic star who inhabited the furthest reaches of the circuitous labyrinth. The Minotaur in my husband's brain has a name, too: Astrocytoma. It is a cancer of the astrocytes, which are star-shaped brain cells that play a supporting role for neurons. Astrocytoma demands the sacrifice of healthy cells to feed its hunger.

It's the day of the second surgery. Along with anesthesia the specialists administer medication that makes tumor cells glow when bathed in blue light. Then they open my husband's head again and reach inside with the aid of a surgical microscope fitted with a tiny blue lamp. Now they can see the horned cells the way ancient artists saw beings emerge on the cave walls, the way Theseus saw the brilliant Minotaur. By seeing the cells clearly, by bringing them into the realm of conscious inspection, the neurosurgeon can understand them and deal with them.

The center is a pivot point, a discovery, a realization. It's not the end of the adventure—you still have to make your way back out—but nothing will be the same again after you encounter the star within.

With the help of that technological blue thread, the medical team does such incredible work that they send my husband home with no further treatment needed. Miracle-drenched, we enter the new labyrinth of recovery knowing nothing of what comes next.

The labyrinth removes us from linearity. It's a bubble that pauses the flow of time and reminds us of the limits of logic and planning. Labyrinths derange our routines and teleport us into the present moment to face our inner starry animals, so shockingly similar to ourselves, potentially so dangerous. But Ariadne presides. She stands ready to help. Her thread turns the labyrinth into the simplest possible map. Just follow the path step by step. The labyrinth itself will lead you.

## REFLECTION QUESTIONS

What labyrinths have you walked, literally or metaphorically? What surprises have you found in the center? How has Ariadne's thread guided you?

## CREATIVE PROMPT: LEAVING THE LABYRINTH

Make a safe space for yourself, whatever that looks like for you. Then give yourself some free time to journal or draw or paint a memory of a time when you made it out of a challenging labyrinth. What messages from this memory come up for you? What inspirations for new creative work? What insights that might help other labyrinth travelers?

**NOTES**

1 Joseph Campbell. *Goddesses: Mysteries of the Feminine Divine*. New World Library, 2013, 101.

2 Thomas G. Palaima. "Appendix One: Linear B Sources." *Anthology of Classical Myth: Primary Sources in Translation*, second edition. Hackett, 2016, 406-407.

3 C. Kerényi. *The Gods of the Greeks*. Thames and Hudson, 1951, 269.

4 Ibid, 110-11.

# ENTERING *the* MYTHSCAPE *of* PAN'S LABYRINTH

*This MythBlast discusses details of the film Pan's Labyrinth, a movie that contains great beauty, graphic violence, and an abundance of what I'll call femme-friendly mythic images. Pan's Labyrinth is rated R.*

*Originally published on March 17, 2024.*

If I could wave a magic wand and invite Joseph Campbell over for dinner tonight, the instant he walked in the door I would sit him down to watch Guillermo del Toro's film *Pan's Labyrinth* (2006). No pleasantries, no chit-chat, no snacks except popcorn and soda, not until he sees the movie. I can already imagine the look on his face when young Ofelia circles down the spiral stone staircase into the realm of the Underground, when the woodland faun first shudders awake, when Ofelia sets out to complete harrowing fairytale tasks to prove her true identity.

Set in rural Spain in 1944, *Pan's Labyrinth* weaves imagery of wonder with images from history, recreating the early years of Franco's fascist rule after the Spanish Civil War. The main character, Ofelia, hovers on the brink of adolescence. Her father died in the war and her mother remarried a cold-blooded captain in Franco's army who embodies the patriarchal brutality of the regime. Ofelia and her mother, who is pregnant with the stepfather's child, move to a remote mill where the captain runs a command post dedicated to wiping out "underground" resistance rebels in the forested hills. But the forest holds a mythic Underground as well as a human one.

Near the end of his life, in the companion book to his televised conversations with Bill Moyers, Campbell mused that movies might function as substitutes for the ritual re-enactments of myth that serve as initiation rites in other cultures, "except that we don't have the same kind of thinking going into the production of a movie that goes into the production of an initiation ritual."[1] Maybe that was the case in the 1980s when Campbell and Moyers created *The Power of Myth*, but *Pan's Labyrinth* presents exactly what Campbell describes: a young woman's passage into adulthood as a mythic initiation into maturity.

When Ofelia first arrives at the mill she is an innocent with a free spirit and a fixation on fairy tales. Wearing a green dress, green coat, and green leather shoes, she follows a flying bug into the forest and then down into the Underground where she meets the faun and undertakes the terrifying tasks that pit her against monsters of many kinds: a giant toad, a cadaverous child-killer with eyes in his hands, and worst of all, her own stepfather. From the toad she learns the power of trickery, from the cadaver she learns to follow her intuition, and from her stepfather she learns who she isn't: she isn't him. She is, instead, someone who will sacrifice herself to protect others, rather than hurting them for her own supposed benefit.

None of these tasks is easy. Initiation never is. But each task teaches Ofelia something vital, something imperative, and by learning these lessons in emotionally charged situations of danger, she changes forever. She is initiated into a new way of being. In this context, the terms *learning, initiation,* and *transformation* are nearly interchangeable. The final scene makes this point by showing the new Ofelia now wearing blood-red: red coat, red shoes, and a dress embroidered with red flowers. Having sacrificed her innocence in her initiation out of virginal, vegetal childhood, she steps into her true identity. The cool greenery of leaves blossoms into the brilliant flowers of her authentic, mature, passionate self.

I grew up in a religion that valued purity, obedience, heaven, and men. Women were literally and spiritually subordinate, a word that means "below ordination." Only men were ordained to religious authority, which meant there were no women in the room when men decided how to run things—from the smallest congregation all the way up to church headquarters— and for guidance the men consulted scriptures full of overt and covert misogyny.

*Pan's Labyrinth,* on the other hand, values dirt, disobedience, earth, and women. For example, Ofelia's confrontation with the toad leaves her covered in mud while the most well-groomed person in the film is the fastidious, hollow-hearted captain. Ofelia learns to follow her intuition and conscience rather than blindly obeying. Instead of a distant heaven, the movie's majestic Underground Realm presents an earth-centered image of the divinity beneath the everyday world containing a trinity of Father, Mother, and Holy Daughter. "You are not born of man," the faun pointedly tells Ofelia,[2] a clear response to the sexist Biblical phrase, "son of man." *Pan's Labyrinth* relocates the sacred away from patriarchy, thereby initiating the viewer into a spiritualized, co-creative vision of gender equality.

Joseph Campbell taught at a progressive women's college for thirty-eight years, from 1934 to 1972. Year after year, from the Great Depression through World War II, the postwar years, the Civil Rights movement, and the Vietnam War, Campbell inspired classrooms full of young women with the transformational possibilities of myth in a time when society hadn't yet allowed them the right to hold credit cards. "All I can tell you about mythology," he writes, "is what men have said and have experienced, and now women have to tell us from their point of view what the possibilities of the feminine future are."[3] Many women have accepted that challenge—before and after Campbell issued it—but what gives me even more hope for gender equality is when men imagine into and champion the experience of women as del Toro does in *Pan's Labyrinth*. With empathy and affection the film portrays complex female characters, exposes the soul-violence of patriarchal oppression, and shows male characters who treat women as honored, beloved equals.

In his interviews with Bill Moyers, Campbell said that the artist's task is "the mythologization of the environment."[4] For Campbell, that would mean shaping some aspect of the world into a narrative, for example Spanish fascism under Franco, then imbuing the narrative with wonder and awe, showing how to cope psychologically with the situation and pointing to the mystery that lies just behind it—in other words, illustrating Campbell's four functions of myth. *Pan's Labyrinth* accomplishes exactly that. Sociologically, the film reveals the brutality of fascist oppression and the possibility of gender equality. Psychologically, Ofelia learns to follow her intuition and conscience rather than blindly obeying outside forces that seek to control her. Cosmologically, an ensouled natural world of beauty and vitality encompasses the built world. Metaphysically, everything springs from the animating source of the Underground Realm, an enchanted font of earth energy that gives rise to all and imbues the world with magic. The faun embodies an especially poignant image of sacred, animate earth. With woody limbs and curving horns, he serves as an earthen-animal-human shaman-priest, facilitating Ofelia's initiation. Del Toro plays a similar role, facilitating the initiation viewers experience.

When the movie ends my imaginary dinner party would move to the kitchen table. Because I have a magic wand I might as well invite del Toro over as well. I'd conjure spaghetti with homemade tomato sauce, fresh bread, olive oil for dipping, and wine to wash it all down. For dessert, walnut brownies with a glossy frosting of melted chocolate and butter—anything to keep my guests talking. So much has happened since *The Power of Myth* and *Pan's Labyrinth* were released. I'd love to hear what the creators of these works have to say about our current mythic moment.

## REFLECTION QUESTIONS

What movie or movies have inspired you deeply? What filmmakers would you most like to sit down and talk with? If you could meet them at a café, what would each of you order?

## CREATIVE PROMPT: IMPOSSIBLE DIALOGUES

Write a scene in the format of a screenplay depicting a conversation between two creative people who inspire you but who never met each other. Include sensory details about flavors, textures, and smells, and lean in on their most passionate points of agreement and disagreement.

## NOTES

1 Joseph Campbell. *The Power of Myth with Bill Moyers*. Anchor, 1991, 102.

2 Guillermo del Toro. Pan's Labyrinth. Warner Brothers, 2006, 00:23:17.

3 Joseph Campbell. *Goddesses: Mysteries of the Feminine Divine*. New World Library, 2013, 263.

4 Joseph Campbell, *The Power of Myth with Bill Moyers*, 107.

# PART 4
# Family Enchantments

# *The* HOUR YIELDS

*By autumn of 2020, the first fall of the Covid-19 pandemic, the whole world seemed to be hovering on a terrifying edge between life and death. That season offered itself to me as a time to write about my father's death, even though he had passed twenty-one years earlier.*

*Originally published on November 29, 2020.*

I don't remember who called with the news that my father had died. I don't remember the conversation. All I remember is the daze in which I found myself putting on a coat, driving to a trailhead, hiking to a cold lookout over the Rio Grande valley.

On the far side of that vast earthen bowl, the slump-shouldered Sangre de Christo Mountains seemed to gaze down into the valley, too. The river etched across the bottom of the bowl as a distant line of bare cottonwood trees, their leaves fallen for winter. Afternoon light tinted the landscape ocher and rose. I sat on a flat tuff rock formed ages ago from volcanic ash. The mountains were still. The mesas, still. The rock, still. My body, still, for the first time since I received the call—

But stillness is not a literal, factual thing. In *The Inner Reaches of Outer Space*, Joseph Campbell points out that the notion of a "still point" doesn't exist in the physical universe.[1] In the field of time and space, there is no cessation of energy, nor any literal, irreducible point. And yet, the cosmos has contrived to create creatures who experience stillness and pointness. The still point is a subjective event, not an objective reality. So, as Campbell says, anywhere can be a still point.[2] I would add that any-when can be a still point, too. We conjure it ourselves. Psyche and imagination collaborate to create still points in our lives—and in myth.

Speaking of Psyche, remember that moment when Psyche first sees her husband by the light of the lamp? She gasps, time stretches, and Psyche falls forever in love with Love, as one does when one marries Eros. Then the sizzling lamp oil lands on Eros's shoulder and the action resumes. Remember when the Minotaur and Theseus catch sight of each other in the torchlit center of the labyrinth? The shock of the other's muscular presence, the instant sizing up, the mutual rush of adrenaline right before they spring at each other to kill or be killed. Demeter realizing that Persephone is gone—*gone*, leaving the Great Mother without her child.

These mythic still points burst with so much emotion that time cannot contain them. The clock stops, the moment opens, the hour yields to make way for hearts that swell past the edges of anything they'd felt or known before into experience so new that their souls must rearrange themselves to make room.

The still point follows the last thing and precedes the next thing. It is the aperture of perception when past and future both hold the baton of awareness. It reverberates with memory and foreknowledge, echoing into eternity.

In this imaginal when-where, the tyranny of duality relaxes its grip. The still point exists between, outside, and all around our paired modes of consciousness—past and future, hidden and revealed, life and death. The still point happens when modes of knowing meet and mingle. They amaze each other, change each other. Both of them realize that they aren't separate at all but instead, they exist within each other. Then a new thing emerges and consciousness expands, growing its field of possibility to include more than it could before.

The still point turns out to be more verb than noun, more spiral than dot, more flow than stasis, more experience than object, more awareness than location. But what is the point of this elusive point? The still point is the when-where in which we notice whatever is there for the noticing. Love. Fury. Awe. Campbell cites Novalis: "The seat of the soul is there, where the outer and inner worlds meet."[3] The still point happens when we occupy the seat of the soul. Every moment of existence offers consciousness and imagination a new point of view, a new vantage. The ever-present, ever-available still point is the when-where in which relationship happens.

—And so, when your father dies, you hover in the still point between his life and his death. Between your family's past and future. Between your life before and your life to come. You float at the threshold between farewell and regret. You mourn what never was but might have been. You become the silent sky that blankets the valley. You become the valley. You become the rock that reaches down into the earth, its back to the sky. You sense the ease with which earth and air welcome him back into themselves, no matter how he might or might not have lived, no matter how you might or might not have responded or understood. All of it is a gift—all of it, and you gather him into yourself at the exact same moment that you let him go.

## REFLECTION QUESTIONS

Recall some moments in your life when time seemed to stop. What do they have in common? How are they different? How are they similar to any scenes from myth?

## CREATIVE PROMPT: MYTHIC MEMOIR

Using any medium that calls to you, tell a story from your life when time seemed to stop as though the story were an ancient myth. Now tell the story of an ancient myth as though it were a memory from your life.

## NOTES

1 Joseph Campbell. *The Inner Reaches of Outer Space: Metaphor as Myth and as Religion*. New World Library, 2002, 3.

2 Ibid, 4.

3 Ibid, 5.

***Follow your bliss***
*means love what you do, have some fun,*
*and change the world to make it*
*more blissful for yourself and others.*

# WHAT *the* CHARIOT CARRIES

*This MythBlast is about my mother, my grandmother, and my great-grandmother. I never met Great-Gramma Jennie, but I've imagined her so many times that she feels like a real person in my life. This one goes out to all the ancestors, with gratitude for the reminder to take afternoon tea breaks.*

*Originally published on July 16, 2023.*

"You're going on a trip," Great-Gramma Jennie told my mother.

Mom was a child then, in the pre-war years of the Great Depression. Grampa and my uncles left during the day for work and school, and Mom stayed home with her mother and her mother's mother, my Great-Gramma Jennie. Every afternoon these three generations—maiden, mother, and crone—paused their work of garden weeding, jam canning, laundry hanging, butter churning, and pie baking to gather at the table for tea.

Loose-leaf green tea it was, brewed in an enameled pot tinted the same pale green as pistachio ice cream. Steam shot from the kettle like destiny, impatient to hear itself discussed, as Gramma poured hot water over the leaves. Then, to Mom's child-sized cup, Gramma added a spoonful of sugar and warmed milk from the family cow. The woody perfume of Grampa's pipe smoke would have lingered in the very floorboards of that kitchen, blending with the aroma of whatever simmered on the stove for supper.

As Gramma and Great-Gramma Jennie drank the hot, grassy tea they chatted about news and neighbors. When they finished Jennie completed the ritual by examining the remaining leaves that flecked the bottom of Mom's cup.

"You're going on a trip," Jennie told her granddaughter every day, peering seriously into the cup as though it were a tiny Holy Grail. "Yes, you're going on a trip."

That was always Mom's future: *you're going on a trip.* If Jennie used tarot for divination instead of tea leaves she might have kept the Chariot card on top of the deck. Portending travel and adventure, the Rider-Waite version of this card shows a rider standing in a chariot harnessed to two full-bosomed sphinxes. But instead of reins the rider holds a scepter.

In *The Hero's Journey: Joseph Campbell on His Life and Work*, Campbell relates the story of the Arthurian knight Parzival who, at one point in his quest for the Grail, rides with the reins slack, letting his horse lead the way. "The horse represents nature power and the rider represents the controlling mind," Campbell says. "The slack reins mean that he's riding nature. His own nature. It's a noble horse who has the same heart as he."[1] Perhaps the Chariot rider, too, has learned to share the same noble heart as the wise-woman sphinxes who give the Chariot its energy and wisdom. The rider exerts the soul's sovereignty, symbolized by the scepter, to let other powers lead, relying on faith and instinct more than control.

*You're going on a trip.* I can imagine Mom's big, green, little-girl eyes shining at this thrilling oracle from her adored Gramma. Jennie's prediction was a blessing, a benison bestowed on a beloved granddaughter. For me, this family story underscores how similar in meaning the words *godmother* and *grandmother* are: wise older women who cherish and gladly work magic on behalf of the youngling.

In 1892, when she was eighteen years old, Jennie spent ten weeks traveling alone by stagecoach-chariot from upstate New York to Boston, and then to the White Mountains of New Hampshire. Her cousin invited her, Jennie later wrote, telling her that "if I came they would take me around and I would see things to think of and tell of in 'future' years and it has proved so. For every night … after I go to bed—it all comes back to me in the quiet hours—of the night—like a moving picture."[2] Jennie's adventure became a lifelong stream of mythic memories. She carried her tales of travel in the chariot of her heart as she moved from maidenhood to motherhood and then into cronedom. When she read Mom's tea leaves, maybe she wished a similar gift for her young granddaughter. That same—or greater—opportunity.

Soon after Jennie's trip, she earned a teacher's certificate and got a job at a school for the children of homesteaders who raised sheep and cows far up a hillside riddled with gullies and streams. To deliver Jennie to that remote village where she lodged with the families of her students, a school trustee gave her a ride up the hill in his wagon-chariot at the beginning of the term and back down again at the end. That steep, forested, rock-pocked trail would have been a bumpy ride indeed, but something about the company must have proved agreeable because before long, Jennie married the trustee and gave birth to my grandmother.

The Chariot carried Jennie to adventure, to her work in the world, to her future family. That's what the Chariot does. It carries. It conveys. The Chariot moves the soul from Point A to Point B faster than that soul could have traveled on its own power.

I imagine Jennie as the rider on the tarot card, standing tall with a twinkle in her eye, holding that scepter of sovereignty, propelled by her own soul's wisdom. I see Gramma as the rider too. I see Mom as the rider. Myself. My whole family. You, if you like. Myth is not only the province of princes and queens. Quiet lives are mythic too.

"You're going on a trip," the Chariot says, and that's how many stories begin: stories of adventure, quest, healing, discovery. "The trip is called your life, and I will carry you anytime you like."

## REFLECTION QUESTIONS

What wisdom and life lessons have you learned from your mother or mothers? From grandmothers? From great-grandmothers?

## CREATIVE PROMPT: YOU'RE GOING ON A TRIP

Go somewhere you've never been before. Temporarily leave behind your normal rhythms and routines, and give yourself the gift of new land and sky, new flavors and fragrances, new ways of being in the world. Notice what insights and ideas arise. When you return home, put something from your experience into a piece of creative work in any medium you like.

**NOTES**

1 Joseph Campbell. The *Hero's Journey: Joseph Campbell on His Life and Work*. New World Library, 1990, 128.

2 Emma Jane Harris Davison. Undated personal reminiscences.

# *To* RADIATE *and* CREATE

*Part of the magic of Joseph Campbell's suggestion to follow your bliss is the word "your." Everyone has their own bliss—or blisses, very likely—and their own ways of following them, but here's a story about what bliss following looked like for me at one point in my life.*

*Originally published on June 23, 2024.*

## LIFE AMONG THE LUMINOUS

As the sixth of seven children I grew up surrounded by people who towered over me and performed feats of astonishing creativity and capacity. My brother was a centaur riding his motorcycle. Dad designed a car wash machine by penciling mysterious schematics of circuitry onto flattened cardboard boxes, as Hephaestus might if he had owned a gas station. Mom floated on air when she executed swan dives into the lake and, in winter, she skated circles around me on the frozen pond behind the house—forward and backward—like a water spirit of the north. My four older sisters drew, painted, baked, photographed, and sewed; they played basketball, softball, and piano; they regaled me with stories they invented on the spot. One sister would materialize as though out of nowhere to hand me magical elixirs—a bottle heated to just the right temperature, a tiny cup of "jello juice" she scooped from the mixing bowl before the liquid gelatin went into the fridge. I can still taste that sweet, warm, red nectar. When my younger sister arrived, she glowed like a divine child with eyes of clear blue quartz and gleaming copper hair.

It all felt miraculous. Stunning. I had blundered into a pantheon of powers greater than myself, and I adored them all, exactly the way I would so many goddesses and gods. With no language to describe it, I was experiencing my family's transparence to transcendence, as Joseph Campbell called it.[1] My child-eyes let me see what Campbell calls "the radiance of the presence of the divine."[2] That radiance shone through my family as though through a cluster of suns.

Unfortunately, I was hopelessly opaque.

## WHEN THE LIGHT DIMS

So there I was, handed from giant to dazzling giant, tossed in the air like a squealing beach ball, spun in circles then set down to fall over in the grass, laughing with giddy dizziness—much the way spiritual experiences leave me feeling. But I had no awareness of my own talents. I couldn't sense Campbell's radiance shining through me.

This luminosity, for Campbell, occurs especially in the experience of art, poetry, myth, and religion[3]—all of which are fields of human creativity. I knew it existed, because I'd seen it from the outside, but I had no experience of it myself. All I had was a desperate desire to participate in the fun everyone else was having.

Before long my siblings started going off to colleges, marriages, jobs, and journeys. I wept at the airport when we dropped them off. It was like I lost God, every single time.

I self-medicated with books—another form of creative marvel which I had no idea how to make. I longed to write stories the way the Brontë sisters did. But no one taught me how, not in high school, not in college. So, after graduating I read about narrative structure. I attended writing classes and conferences. I joined writing groups, and I wrote awful stories—one after another after another.

Ten full years of this went by, and then one day I came across Ray Bradbury's book *Zen in the Art of Writing*, in which he describes writing one story a week, every week.[4] Well, I though, why not try that? Nothing else had worked, so I rolled up my sleeves.

The first week, I wrote a horrible story.

The second week, another horrible story.

Weeks three, four, five, and six: terrible story after terrible story.

My settings lacked vitality. Plots petered out. Characters lay flat on the page, stubbornly refusing to stand up and do anything. Looking back, I must have been as stubborn as they were. My grim determination would not let me give up, no matter how much I despaired over each failure.

## STUBBORNNESS, MEET SURRENDER

In the seventh week of my Bradbury challenge, I had a vague idea for a character and setting. The first few pages filled up decently well, but the middle slowed down. Words dried to a trickle. Then they stopped. I had no idea what came next.

It was on a Thursday, just past sunset—late in the day, late in the week, late in my soul. Why was I unable to write a story? None of my siblings would struggle like this, not with their array of talents. But it was time to make supper, so I gave up. This story would be another swing and a miss.

I turned off my computer and trudged down the shadowy staircase from my office to the kitchen letting gravity do most of the work. Downstairs, the windows were squares of the evening's deepening blue, the furniture all but invisible in the dark.

As I stepped off the last stair I flipped the switch for the kitchen lights as I always did. Unlike other times, though, this time when the kitchen lit up, *so did the story's ending.*

There it was in my mind, all at once, and it was perfect. Perfect! I loved it! Surprising yet inevitable, it fit the previous pages like a key in a lock, and *I had not invented it.* The story's ending arrived in my mind all on its own at the same moment as that burst of light. Electrical light and story light flooded me both at once, accompanied by a feeling of indescribable joy and impossible delight—wordless, timeless, thrilling, alive. If a camera had recorded that moment it might have captured eureka photons beaming from my ears, somewhere on the light spectrum just this side of indigo.

The radiance. The divine.

Still breathless, I wrote up the ending. That was my first published story.

But while I edited I was looking over my shoulder. Who or what had come up with that ending? It certainly wasn't me.

## A CREATIVITY CREDO

I was thirty-five when that story's ending burst in and lit up my imagination. That's thirty-five trips around the sun before I found a situation where Campbell's creative radiance could shine through. Afterwards it became more accessible. That's why I believe creativity can be cultivated. But chasing the mystery of how that insight happened became more urgent for me than writing more stories. The embodied sensation of light was so overwhelming, so benefic, that I found myself in graduate school learning about creativity and creation myth.

I never fully solved the mystery, and I never will, but I learned that creation myths represent creativity metaphorically, masking the radiance in stories about forces that pour into the world, stop us in our tracks, and sometimes break through in experiences of art, myth, and religion. I believe Campbell is right that mythic images represent our spiritual potential, and encountering them can activate those potentials in our lives.[5] If goddesses and gods embody and evoke cosmic powers, creator deities embody and evoke creativity. And because creator deities are sacred, so is creativity.

My siblings remain bathed in wonder to me. I'll never stop trying to earn my place among them. I have come to believe their exploits were, in fact, so many acts of God, and I believe our birthright—yours, mine, and everyone's—is to radiate and create.

## REFLECTION QUESTIONS

What do you believe about creativity? What do you believe about your own creativity? Would you like to change any of those beliefs? If so, what would changing that belief require, and what would you like to believe instead?

## CREATIVE PROMPT: SEVEN-DAY CHALLENGE

Choose a type of creative work that you would like to engage with more deeply—storytelling, poetry, sketching, collage, singing, or anything else at all—and commit to spending time practicing that craft every day for seven days, even if only fifteen minutes. If you keep a journal, record how the experience changes your work and your feelings about it.

### NOTES

1 Joseph Campbell. The *Hero's Journey: Joseph Campbell on His Life and Work*. New World Library, 1990, 51.

2 Joseph Campbell. *The Power of Myth with Bill Moyers*. Anchor, 1991, 267.

3 Ibid , 277, 283, 259, 285.

4 Ray Bradbury. *Zen in the Art of Writing*. Bantam, 1992, 67-68.

5 Joseph Campbell, *Power of Myth*, 273.

# Afterword

The essays in this book were originally published by the Joseph Campbell Foundation as part of the Foundation's weekly MythBlast series. Each essay has been lightly edited for inclusion here.

My heartfelt gratitude goes to all my colleagues at the Foundation, current and former, who made this work possible through their generous gifts of opportunity, inspiration, editing, collaboration, and friendship. I especially want to thank John Bucher, Bradley Olson, Stephanie Zajchowski, Stephen Gerringer, Michael Lambert, Tyler Lapkin, Torri Yates-Orr, Scott Neumeister, Jason Batt, Dylan Treadwell, Teddy Hamstra, Jimmy Maxwell, and Bob Walter. Thank you for enchanting my world and the worlds of so many others!

# About Joseph Campbell

Joseph Campbell was an American author and teacher best known for his work in the field of comparative mythology. He was born in New York City in 1904, and from early childhood he became interested in mythology. He loved to read books about Indigenous American cultures, and frequently visited the American Museum of Natural History in New York, where he was fascinated by the museum's collection of totem poles. Campbell was educated at Columbia University, where he specialized in medieval literature, and, after earning a master's degree, continued his studies at universities in Paris and Munich. While abroad he was influenced by the art of Pablo Picasso and Henri Matisse, the novels of James Joyce and Thomas Mann, and the psychological studies of Sigmund Freud and Carl Jung. These encounters led to Campbell's theory that all myths and epics are linked in the human psyche, and that they are cultural manifestations of the need to explain social, cosmological, and spiritual realities.

After a period in California where he encountered John Steinbeck and the biologist Ed Ricketts, Campbell taught at the Canterbury School and then, in 1934, joined the literature department at Sarah Lawrence College, a post he retained for many years. During the 1940s and '50s, he helped Swami Nikhilananda to translate the Upaniṣads and *The Gospel of Sri Ramakrishna*. He also edited works by the German scholar Heinrich Zimmer on Indian art, myths, and philosophy. In

1944, with Henry Morton Robinson, Campbell published *A Skeleton Key to Finnegans Wake*. His first original work, *The Hero with a Thousand Faces*, came out in 1949 and was immediately well received; in time, it became acclaimed as a classic. In this study of the "myth of the hero," Campbell asserted that there is a single pattern of heroic journey and that all cultures share this essential pattern in their various heroic myths. In his book he also outlined the basic conditions, stages, and results of the archetypal hero's journey.

Joseph Campbell died in 1987. In 1988, a series of television interviews, *Joseph Campbell and the Power of Myth with Bill Moyers*, introduced Campbell's views to millions of people.

# ABOUT *the* AUTHOR

Joanna Gardner, PhD is a writer, mythologist, and magical realist. Her research and teaching focus on creativity, goddesses, and wonder tales. Joanna serves as director of marketing and communications for the Joseph Campbell Foundation and is the lead author of the Foundation's book, *Goddesses: A Skeleton Key Study Guide.* She teaches in Pacifica Graduate Institute's Mythological Studies program, and is a co-founder of the Fates and Graces community of mythologists. To read Joanna's blog and additional publications, you are most cordially invited to visit her website at joannagardner.com.

# ABOUT *the* JOSEPH CAMPBELL FOUNDATION

The Joseph Campbell Foundation (JCF) is a not-for-profit corporation that continues the work of Joseph Campbell, exploring the fields of mythology and comparative religion. The Foundation is guided by three principal goals:

First, the Foundation preserves, protects, and perpetuates Campbell's pioneering work. This includes cataloging and archiving his works, developing new publications based on his works, directing the sale and distribution of his published works, protecting copyrights to his works, and increasing awareness of his works by making them available in digital format on JCF's website.

Second, the Foundation promotes the study of mythology and comparative religion. This involves implementing and/or supporting diverse mythological education programs, supporting and/or sponsoring events designed to increase public awareness, donating Campbell's archived works, and utilizing JCF's website as a forum for relevant cross-cultural dialogue.

Third, the Foundation helps individuals enrich their lives by experiencing the power of myth through community outreach and periodic Joseph Campbell–related events and activities.

Joseph Campbell Foundation

www.jcf.org

John Bucher, Executive Director

Bradley Olson, Director of Publications

Printed in the USA
CPSIA information can be obtained
at www.ICGtesting.com
CBHW040947181124
17427CB00067B/857